Who's in That Barn?

Author and Illustrations by:

Marybeth Fetters

Author and Illustrator: Marybeth Fetters (Tucker - Hess)
(MB)
explorewithmbf@gmail.com
2020-2023

ISBN #979-8-218-17362-3

"Be your awesome self"

Dedication:

Big thanks to all my family, friends, ranchers and farmers. I've learned to explore different paths in my life, and you all gave me the courage to be... "Be your awesome self."

Who's in
that barn?

Cow!

The Cow says,

"Moo Moo".

A baby cow is called a

Calf.

Who's in
that barn?

Pig!

The Pig says,

"Oink Oink".

A baby pig is called a

Piglet.

Who's in
that barn?

Sheep!

The Sheep says,

"Baa Baa".

A baby sheep is called a **Lamb.**

Who's in
that barn?

Cat!

The Cat says,

"Meow Meow".

A baby cat is called a

Kitten.

Who's in
that barn?

Chicken!

The Chicken says,

"Cluck Cluck".

A baby chicken
is called a

Chick.

Who's in
that barn?

Goat!

The Goat says,

"Maa Maa".

A baby goat is called a **Kid.**

Who's in
that barn?

Horse!

The Horse says,

"Neigh Neigh".

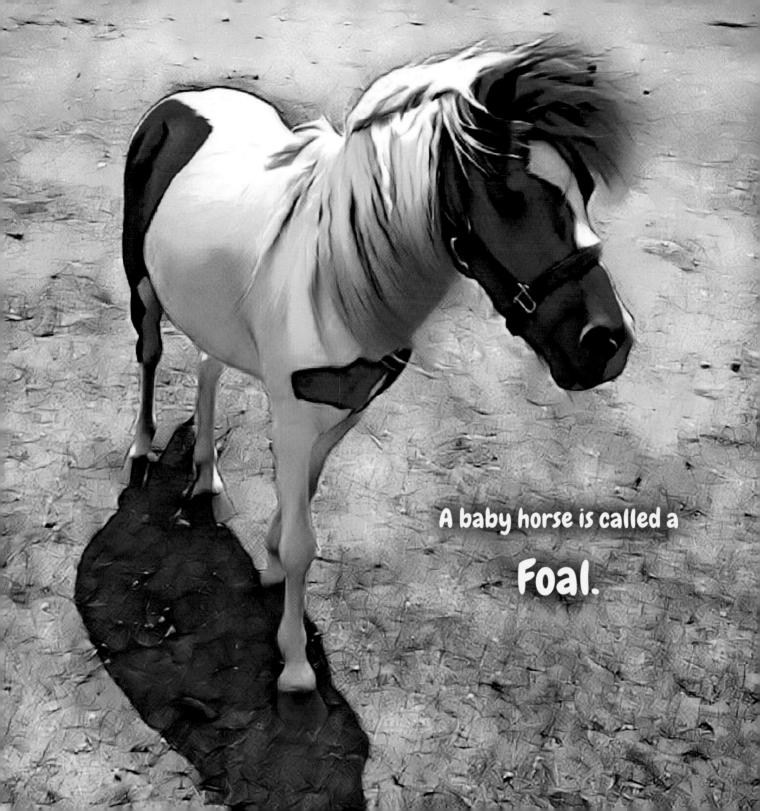

A baby horse is called a

Foal.

The End!

Fun Facts

* Cows give us milk.

* Cows (Cattle) Mother's (Female) are called Cows.

* Father's (Male) are called Bulls.

* Pigs (Swine) Mother's (Female) are called Sow.

* Father's (Male) are called Boar.

* Sheep give us wool.

* Sheep Mother's (Female) are called Ewe.

* Father's (Male) are called Ram.

* Cats Mother's (Female) are called Queen.

* Father's (Male) are called Tomcat.

* Chickens give us eggs.

* Chickens Mother's (Female) are called Hen.

* Father's (Male) are called Rooster.

* Goats give us milk.

* Goats Mother's (Female) are called Nanny.

* Father's (Male) are called Billy.

* Horses Mother's (Female) are called Mare.

* Father's (Male) are called Stallion.

* Some of these Barns are from the 1800's. Barns then and now are multi-purpose structures. They house livestock, such as cows, horses, and chickens in lower levels, while the upper levels were used for storing hay, grain, and farm equipment.

Author Bio:

Marybeth Fetters

She grew up in Indiana with her Mom, Dad, 2 brothers and 3 sisters. She is always creative, doodling on paper and drawing something. She enjoys books, because in books she can use her imagination. She learned at a young age she had a learning disability. It never held her back, she was encouraged by her family and teachers.

Having adult Dyslexia is a gift not a disability. Her success is baby steps, and she knew comprehending things would be different in her mind. She would see a picture in her mind, not words. She would think in images as opposed to words.

Looking back on growing up, she remembers visiting her Aunt's farm and thinking how it inspired her to write this book. She learned to explore the farm life and her love for all animals.

Now she lives in a little Village in Michigan, surrounded by lots of farmland. She lives with her husband and her cat, Toby. She has two adult sons and one daughter. She has two wonderful grandsons, one son-in-law and two stepsons.

Always encouraging ... **"Be your awesome self"**.